COMPUTERS
OUR LIFELINE

1

MANOJ PUBLICATIONS

COMPUTERS
Our Lifeline -1

Publisher

MANOJ PUBLICATIONS

761, Main Road, Burari, Delhi-110084
Ph.   : 27611116, 27611349
Fax   : 27611546, (M) : 9868112194
email   : info@manojpublications.com
Website : manojpublications.com

Showroom :

1583-84, Dariba Kalan, Chandni Chowk, Delhi-110006
Ph. : 23262174, 23268216
Mobile : 9818753569

ISBN 978-81-310-1639-8

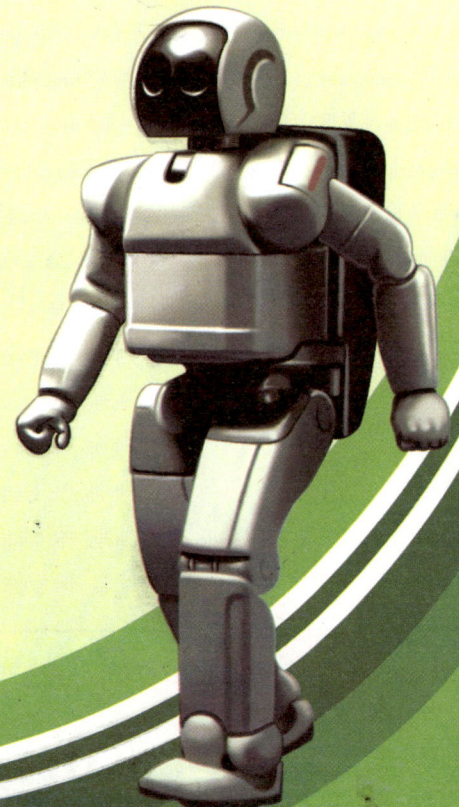

Concept:
Puneet Gupta
M.B.A. (William & Mary, U.S.A.)

Edited by:
Davinder Singh Minhas

PREFACE

This is the age of computers. In every nook and corner of the globe, computers have made their presence felt, be it school, office, post office, bank, shop, mall, hotel, restaurant, airport, railway station, metro station and so on. Needless to say, they have become our lifeline, as we can't do anything without them. In order to keep pace with the modern world it is important to familiarise our children with computer applications right from the start. They ought to be taught the uses of computer in a lucid, interesting and enjoyable style: from basic to intermediate to advanced level.

Keeping in view the requirements of students, all the books in the series—Computers: Our Lifeline—have been designed to meet the purpose of acquiring a sound in-depth knowledge on computers with their uses. The contents of the books are based entirely on CCE (Continuous and Comprehensive Evaluation).

The chapters in all the books contain a fairly good amount of illustrations which make the text very easy to understand. There are many computer books flooding the market. Our books are the books with a difference in order that they are well equipped with exhaustive exercises which test a student's mental horizon by making him take Formative Assessment as well as Summative Assessment. The main goal of books in the series is to make a student computerate, *i.e.* computer literate.

We sincerely hope that all the books in this series will prove fruitful both to students and teachers. We shall be highly pleased to receive constructive suggestions in order to make the series more qualitative in the forthcoming editions.

—Author

Contents

1 INTRODUCTION TO COMPUTERS

Hi kids ! My name is 'Comp'.
I am a **computer**. I am your friend.
I shall help you to learn and understand
about me in a very easy way. So let's be
friends. Ready, Steady and Go………………………

Wow ! You are looking very smart. Tell me something about yourself.

I am an **electronic machine;** I can do many things for you.

WHAT IS A MACHINE?

A **machine** is a device which is made by **man**. It makes our work easier, faster and better.

Let me explain you.

Friends, there are two kinds of machines:

(1) Manual machines

(2) Electronic machines

A typewriter is a **manual** machine.

I am an **electronic** machine.

- **Manual machines** are run by **man**. They do not require electricity to work.

- **Electronic machines** are run on **electricity**. They require electricity to work.

Friends, before moving ahead, let me check what you have learnt till now.

Here are the machines, you have **seen** in your home. **Tick [✓]** whether it is **manual** or **electronic**.

Manual Machine	☐	Electronic Machine ☐
Manual Machine	☐	Electronic Machine ☐
Manual Machine	☐	Electronic Machine ☐
Manual Machine	☐	Electronic Machine ☐
Manual Machine	☐	Electronic Machine ☐

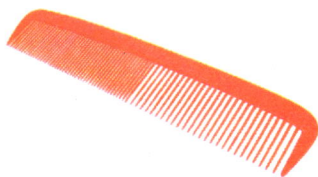

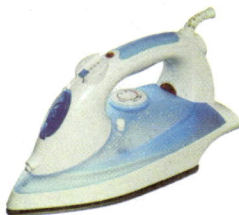

Computers—Our Lifeline-1

DIFFERENT TYPES OF MACHINES

There are many types of machines that help you in one way or the other.

Machines help you to **move**.

Car

Cycle

Bike

Machines help you to do **work** easier at home.

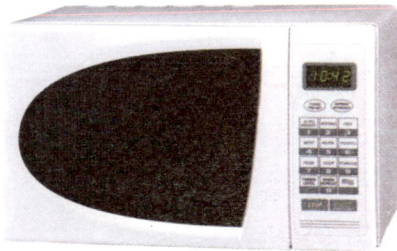
Microwave oven

Vacuum cleaner

Phone

Machines **entertain** you.

Television

Music system

Video Game

So like other machines, I am also an **electronic machine** that can do many things and make your work easier and faster. Let's have a look at what I can do.

Computer

- I can draw pictures.
- I can show you a cartoon movie.
- I can sing a song.
- I can count numbers.
- I can play games.
- I can remember many things.

So, you have come to know about me and what I can do for you. Let's be good friends now.

LET'S HAVE A LOOK

○ A computer is an electronic machine.

○ A machine is a device made by man.

○ Manual machines and Electronic machines are two kinds of a machine.

○ Machines help you to move and entertain.

FUN TIME

1. Here are some pictures of the machines. Write 'M' if it is Manual and 'E' if it is Electronic.

2. Tick [✓] the correct pictures shown below.

a. Your father wants to reach office quickly. Should he go:

by Car   □

□   **on foot**

b. Your mother wants to clean the home without getting tired; she should use a:

Broom   □

□   **Vacuum Cleaner**

c. Your friend wants to go on the sixth floor of the mall quickly. Should he use:

Stairs   □

□   **An Escalator**

d. Your brother wants to reach college quickly. Should he go by:

Bike   □

□   **Cycle**

BRAIN TEASER

1. **Write the first letter of each of the given pictures in the writing space with the help of the words given below.**

    Orange, cat, rose, tomato, monkey, umbrella, elephant, horse, apple, pen, ice cream, nest

C	O						

2. **Can you correct my spelling?**

    a. | A | M | C | I | H | S | N | E |

    b. | L | C | E | T | E | O | I | C | N | R |

3. **Guess the machine:**

   a. It gives you ice.

   | R | F | | | | | A | | R |

   b. It flies high in the sky.

   | A | | O | | | N | E |

   c. We watch movies on it.

   | T | L | | | | I | N |

   d. It can do a lot of work.

   | C | M | | | | R |

4. **Write the following numbered letters of the English alphabet (A, B, C, ..., Z).**

   3rd   15th   13th   16th   21st   20th   5th   18th

   _____ _____ _____ _____ _____ _____ _____ _____

5. **Tick [✓] the correct answer and cross [✗] the incorrect one.**

   a. A computer is a manual machine. ☐

   b. Machines make our work difficult. ☐

   c. A car is a machine. ☐

   d. A computer can do calculations very fast. ☐

   e. A computer is very obedient. ☐

   f. A computer is a man-made machine. ☐

ACTIVITY TIME

Join these dots numberwise and see what comes in front of you. Colour it as well.

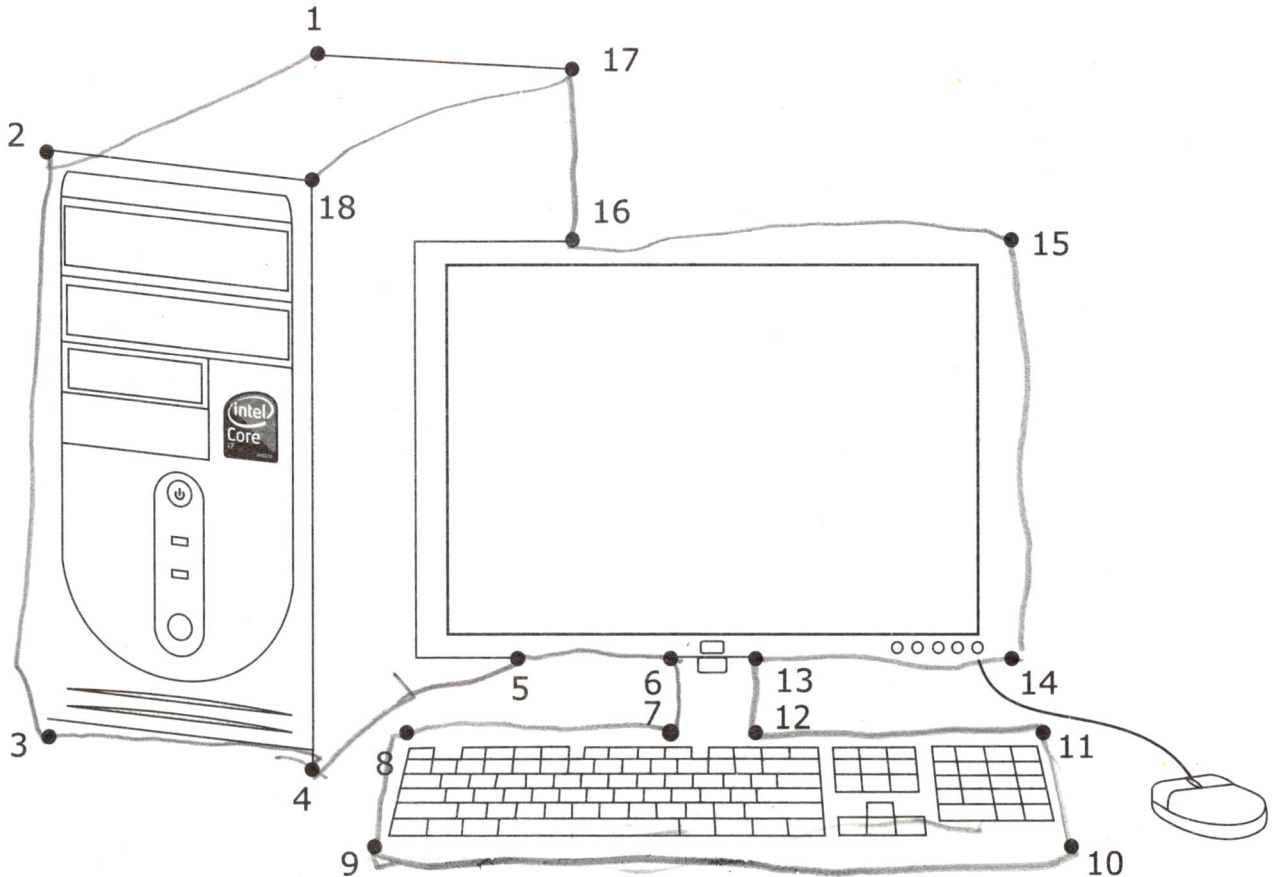

So, tell me who I am.

c	a	m	p	u	t	e	R

LAB ACTIVITY

The teacher will take students to the computer lab and make them familiar with the computer. Show them the functions of the different parts of the computer.

Hello friends! I am back again to tell you more about myself.

Hello Comp! We are also ready to learn.

There are many tasks that I can do for you.

What are those tasks ?

OK friends, let's have a look.

FUNCTIONS OF A COMPUTER

As you all know, being a smart machine, I can do various things for you.

1. You can write letters, words and numbers on the computer.

2. You can work out different sums quickly and easily on the computer.

2. You can play different types of games on the computer.

Computers—Our Lifeline-1

4. You can listen to music and other sounds from the speakers attached to the computer.

5. You can watch movies and cartoons on the computer.

6. You can draw and colour pictures on the computer.

Let's Get Friends

7. You can send messages to your friends anywhere in the world within a few seconds.

FEATURES OF A COMPUTER

Fast Speed

1. A Computer works at a very fast **speed**. You can do your work very quickly.

2. A Computer can do many types of work altogether at the same time.

3. A Computer never makes a mistake and always gives you a correct answer.

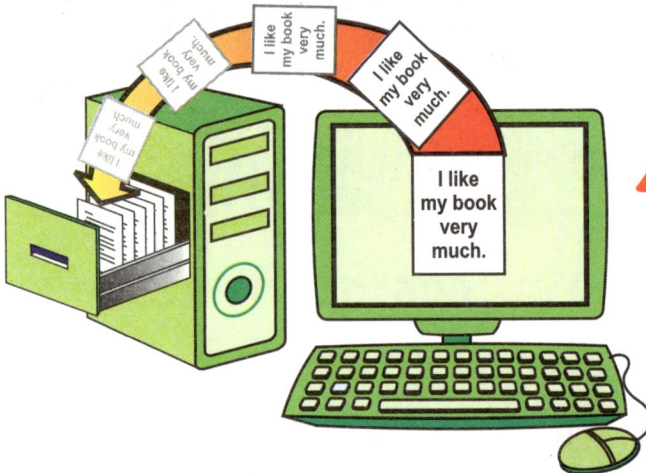

100 % MARKS

4. A Computer can remember lots of things for a long time.

I like my book very much.

So, one computer and many tasks. It is like the magical machine that can do anything for you.

LET'S HAVE A LOOK

- A Computer can do various things for you.

- A Computer works at a very fast speed.

- It can draw and paint.

- It can show you a movie and a cartoon movie.

- You can type words, sentences and numbers on it.

- You can listen to music on it.

FUN TIME

A Computer is a single machine and does many tasks for you. Tick [✓] the pictures of machines whose work can also be done on the computer.

BRAIN TEASER

1. **Tick [✓] the correct answer.**

   a. The speed of a computer is very (**fast**/slow).

   b. The computer can do (**many**/one) types of work at the same time.

   c. The computer (**can**/cannot) remember things.

   d. The computer (**never**/can) makes mistakes.

   e. You (**can**/cannot) play music on a computer.

2. **Write 'T' for true and 'F' for false in the boxes given below.**

   a. A Computer can work out mathematical sums. `T`

   b. A Computer cannot draw a colour picture. `F`

   c. A Computer cannot write letters or numbers. `F`

   d. A Computer can wash your clothes. `F`

   e. A Computer cannot remember things. `F`

   f. A Computer can show you a cartoon movie . `T`

   g. A Computer cannot work fast. `F`

   h. A Computer can send messages. `T`

3. **Match each of the following pictures with the activity.**

Typing words

Playing games

Watching movies

Doing sums

Listening to music

LAB ACTIVITIES

1. Show students the different tasks done by computer like painting, calculating, listening to songs, etc.

2. Show how a computer is different from other machines.

FORMATIVE ASSESSMENT - 1
Chapters 1 and 2

1. Tick [✓] the objects that are machines.

✓	✓	✓
(typewriter)	(dog)	(bicycle)
	✓	
(rose)	(comb)	(car)
	✓	
(broom)	(telephone)	(ladder)

2. Look at the picture and tell what the computer is doing for you.

_____ _____ _____
_____ _____ _____
_____ _____ _____

Hello friends ! As you know, I can do a variety of tasks. For doing all these tasks I am being used at different places. Now I shall tell you where you can see me.

AT HOME

The computer is used:
- to do your homework
- to draw and colour pictures
- to play games
- to watch movies
- to use the Internet

IN OFFICE

The computer is used:
- to type and print letters
- to do calculations
- for keeping records
- to send and receive messages

IN BANKS

The computer is used:

- o to deposit and withdraw the money
- o to maintain the accounts
- o to use an ATM

IN SHOPS

The computer is used:
- o for making bills
- o to keep the record of goods

AT RAILWAY STATION / AIRPORTS

The computer is used:

- o for reserving tickets and seats
- o for keeping the records of passengers
- o for guiding the route to the pilot

AT SCHOOLS

The computer is used:

- for teaching
- for keeping the records of students and teachers
- for keeping the fee record
- for preparing the results

IN THE HOSPITAL

The computer is used:

- for helping the doctor to diagnose diseases
- for keeping the records of patients

IN FACTORIES

The computer is used:

- to make different things
- for running machines

- A computer helps in many areas.

- It helps in a school, shop, hospital and an office.

- It helps in an airport and a railway station.

FUN TIME

Here are the pictures. Guess and write the place where the computer is being used.

BRAIN TEASER

1. **Complete the name of the area where a computer:**

   a. Helps make bills.

S		P	

   b. Helps in the reservation of tickets.

A			O	T

   c. Helps keep the record of patients.

H		P		T		L

   d. Helps teach students.

S		H		L

   e. Helps print documents.

O		F			E

2. **Tick [✓] the correct answer.**

   a. At home, a computer can be used to watch a

      1. Cartoon Movie ◯   2. Bills ◯

   b. In offices, computers can be used for typing

      1. Poems ◯   2. Letters ◯

   c. In schools, computers are used for preparing

      1. accounts ◯   2. results ◯

   d. In factories, computers are used for running

      1. machines ◯   2. records ◯

3. **Write 'T' for true or 'F' for false in the boxes given below.**

a.   A computer cannot be used at shops. ☐

b.   A computer helps at a railway station. ☐

c.   A computer can keep the fee record at school. ☐

d.   A computer cannot do printing in offices. ☐

e.   A computer is used for teaching. ☐

LAB ACTIVITY

Visit all the places in your school and see the working of a computer at each place.

FUN ACTIVITY

Visit any mall or shop and watch the work of computers there. Get a bill from there and paste it in the box given below.

Hi friends! As your body have different parts I have also different parts. In this chapter, I shall be telling you about some of my main parts.

PARTS OF A COMPUTER

But before telling you about my parts, I want to give you a small test.

Can you name some of your body-parts?

Oh ! smart kids. You know all about your body-parts.

Kids, each and every part in your body has some specific task to do.

Just like your body-parts, I have different parts which have some specific tasks to do.

The Computer mainly has **four** parts.

1. CPU   **2.** Monitor   **3.** Keyboard   **4.** Mouse

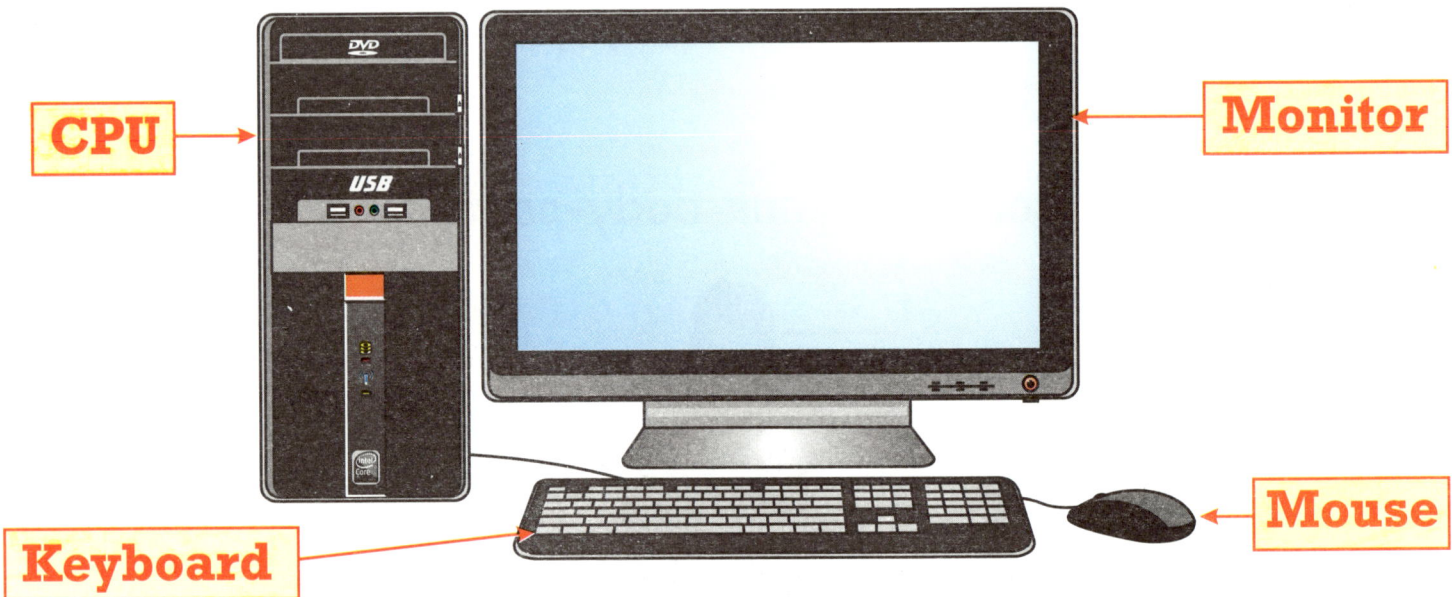

CPU

Monitor

Keyboard

Mouse

All these four parts connected together make a **computer system**. Each part has its own use.

Now, let us learn about the use of each of its four parts.

Monitor

Meet this part of me. This is **Monitor**.

- A monitor looks like a TV-screen.

- We can see words, pictures, cartoons and stories on this monitor.

- All the work we do on the computer comes on the monitor.

Keyboard

This is a **keyboard**.

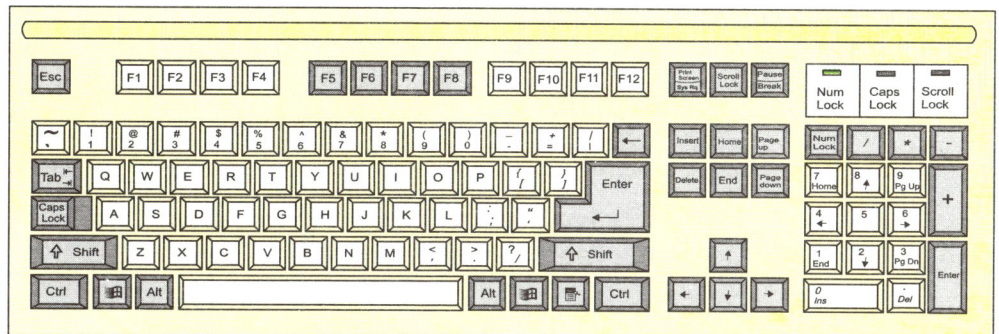

- A keyboard is used to type words and numbers into the computer.

- It has small buttons on it called **keys**.

CPU

CPU stands for Central Processing Unit.

- CPU is the **brain** of the computer.

- CPU controls the functions of all other parts of the computer, just like a brain.

- CPU does all types of calculations in the computer.

Mouse

This is a **mouse**. A Mouse has a small body and a long tail.

But it is not a real mouse that you see at home. It is a computer mouse.

- A Mouse is a **pointing device**.

- A Mouse is used to draw and colour pictures and play games.

- It is also used to select objects on a **computer** screen.

LET'S HAVE A LOOK

○ Like our body-parts, a computer has also different parts.
○ Monitor, keyboard, CPU and mouse are the four main parts of the computer.
○ A Monitor looks like a T.V.-screen.
○ A Keyboard has small buttons called keys.
○ CPU is the brain of the computer.
○ A Mouse is used to paint, draw and play games.

FUN TIME

1. Colour the parts of the computer and write the names.

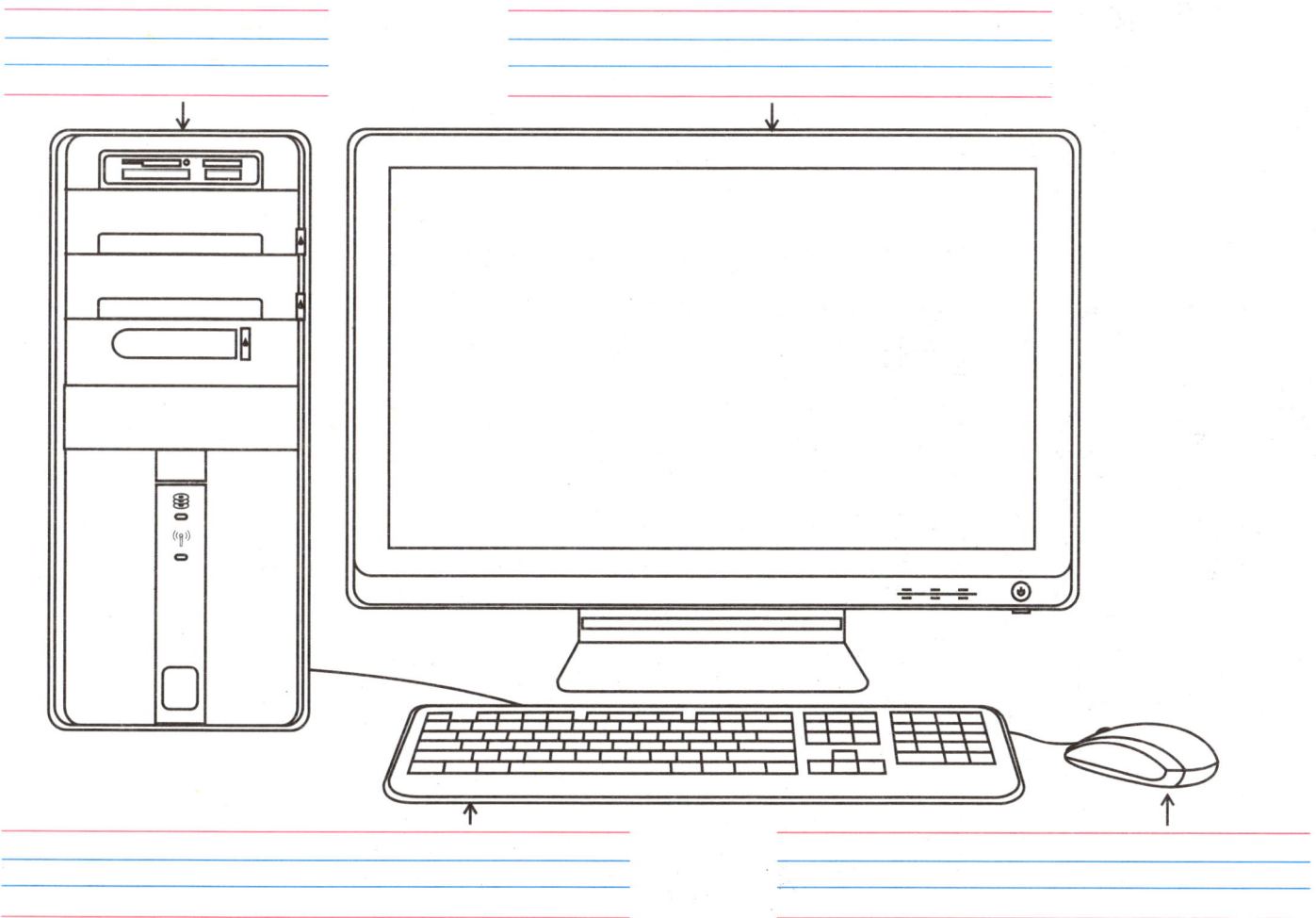

2. The Keyboard wants to meet the other parts of the computer. Help the keyboard to make a complete computer system.

BRAIN TEASER

1. Match the symbols to find the parts of the computer.

☺	✿	◗	✠	✡	☯	✤	⌘	◎	✦	⌑	⇕	⇝	☉	☐	✈
O	M	I	N	E	A	R	T	C	U	S	B	D	P	K	Y

✿	☺	✦	⌑	✡
M				

☐	✡	✈	⇕	☺	☯	✤	⇝

✿	☺	✠	◗	⌘	☺	✤

◎	☉	✦

34

2. **Decode to find the parts of the computer.**

a. _____ = _____

b. 🔑 + **BACK To School** = _____

c. 🏞 + P + YOU = _____

3. **Rearrange the jumbled words to find the names of the computer parts.**

a. | U | P | C | _____

b. | A | R | D | O | B | Y | K | E | _____

c. | T | M | O | N | O | R | I | _____

d. | U | S | M | E | O | _____

4. Fill in the blanks using the given words in the box.

> Mouse,   Keyboard,   CPU,   Monitor

a. _____ is called the brain of the computer.

b. We type words with the help of the _____

c. A _____ is used to select objects.

d. Whatever you work you see on the _____

5. Match the following:

a.      ●   ● Mouse

b.      ●   ● CPU

c.      ●   ● Keyboard

d.      ●   ● Monitor

ACTIVITY TIME

Find the missing part of the computer and write its name in the blank.

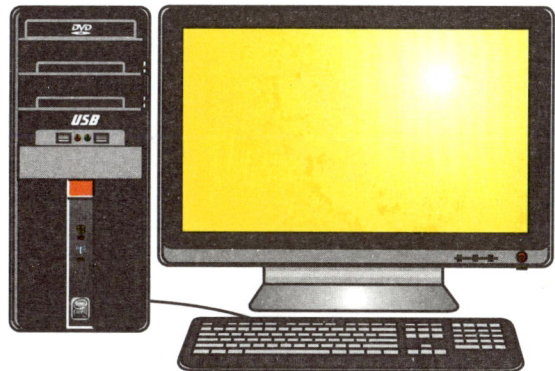

LAB ACTIVITY

Visit your Computer Lab and write the exact number of CPUs, monitors, mouses and keyboards.

CPU .... Monitors ....

Mouses .... Keyboards ....

1. Match each of the computer parts with the function it does.

    a.   ●   ● Typing Words

    b.   ●   ● Drawing Pictures

    c.   ●   ● Doing Calculations

    d.   ●   ● Watching Cartoons

2. Draw the missing parts of the computer.

SUMMATIVE ASSESSMENT - 1
Chapters 1 to 4

A. Answer the following:

1. Name two types of machines.

2. Write two things you can do with the computer.

3. Name any two parts of the computer.

4. Name two areas where you can see the computer.

B. Find out the following words from the puzzle.

KEYBOARD   MONITOR   CALCULATOR

COMPUTER   CPU   OFFICE

C	C	A	L	C	U	L	A	T	O	R
K	B	D	C	K	A	A	Q	C	B	P
E	S	M	O	N	I	T	O	R	C	R
Y	F	K	M	O	P	R	K	C	P	U
B	L	E	P	O	N	M	C	T	D	S
O	U	U	U	S	B	U	O	T	L	K
A	G	T	T	O	F	F	I	C	E	
R	V	X	E	R	T	O	F	T	K	M
D	H	Z	R	I	U	J	T	R	S	Y

Hey friends! In the previous chapter, you learnt about my different parts. Now, I shall tell you how to use these parts. Let's do it one by one.

In this chapter, you will learn about the **keyboard**. It is one of the major parts of the computer.

KEYBOARD

As you use a **pencil** to write on **paper**, in the same way you use the **keyboard** to write in the **computer screen**.

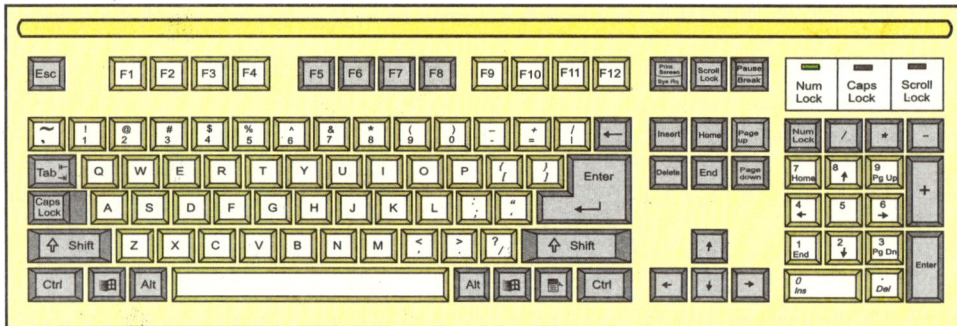

A **keyboard** is a rectangular board that has many **small buttons** on it. These buttons are called **keys**.

You can **type** text on the computer by pressing these keys. **Pressing** the keys of the keyboard is called **typing**.

TYPES OF KEYS ON KEYBOARD

There are many keys on the keyboard such as:

Alphabet Keys

The keys from **A — Z** are called **alphabet keys**.

You can type **words** and **sentences** with the help of these alphabet keys.

Alphabet keys

OK! just count and write how many alphabet keys there are.

Number of Alphabet keys =

Yes, there are **26 keys** of the **English alphabet**, which are marked A, B, C,.... Z on them. These keys are not arranged in the **alphabetical** order.

Number keys

Number keys are marked with the digits 1, 2, ... 9 and 0 on them.

You can type **numbers** with the help of these keys.

OK! just count and write how many number keys there are.

Number of Number keys =

Yes, there are **10** number keys on the keyboard. You can type your **phone number** and **date** with these number keys.

For example, to type **2014**, you press:

Special Keys

There are some other keys on the keyboard that are used for some special work like:

Spacebar key

Spacebar is the **longest** key on the keyboard.

Spacebar is used to give a **blank space** between two words.

If you want to type a sentence on monitor

I love my computer.
space

the **space** between the words is given by **spacebar**.

First press **I** then press **Spacebar** then type **love** then press **Spacebar** then type **my** then press **Spacebar** then type **computer**. This way, you are able to type a complete sentence with proper space.

Enter Key

While typing, **Enter key** is used to move the **cursor** to the next line. Enter key is also called **Return Key**.

There are **two** Enter keys on the keyboard.

What is a cursor ?

A **cursor** is a blinking line | on the screen.

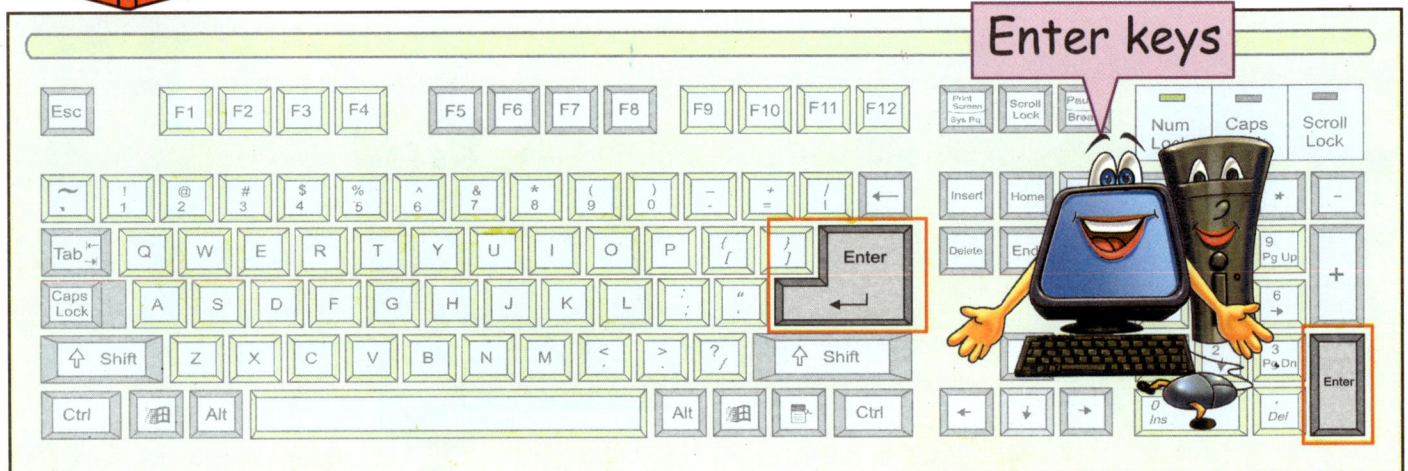

Enter keys

You want to type a sentence on the monitor.

I love my computer.

Now you want to write your name below in a new line.

Press the **Enter** key after the word **computer**. Then type **your name**. You will see on the screen as:

I love my computer.
Davinder Singh

Backspace key

Backspace key is used to erase the characters you just typed wrong from the keyboard.

Backspace erases from the **left** side of the **cursor**.

I love my ~~common tree~~.
I love my country.

If you do not want to write 'common tree', you can erase this on the computer with the help of **BACKSPACE** key.

OK! just place the **cursor** on the last word.

I love my common tree.| ←——— Press [←] key.

I love my| ←——— Press [←] key again, until you delete the desired text.

I love my |country. ┌ Start writing the text again.

Caps Lock key

A **Caps Lock key** is used to type the letters in lowercase or uppercase.

It is a **toggle** key; means if the Caps Lock is **ON** you can type capital letters and if it is **OFF** you can type small letters.

It has a **light** on the top-right corner of the keyboard

So friends, these are some of the very important keys of the keyboard. You will learn more about the keys in the next class.

H A V E   A   N I C E   D A Y

LET'S HAVE A LOOK

- A Keyboard is used to type in the computer.
- It has small buttons on it called keys.
- Alphabet keys are used to type words and letters.
- Number keys are used to type numbers.
- Backspace key is used to erase the character.
- Enter key is used to move the cursor to the next line.
- Spacebar key is used to give space between two words.

FUN TIME

Here is the keyboard. Look at the computer keyboard and fill in the missing keys and colour them.

Alphabet Keys - Red   ●   Number Keys - Yellow ●

Enter Keys - Green   ●   Caps Lock - purple   ●

Backspace Key - Orange ●   Spacebar - blue   ●

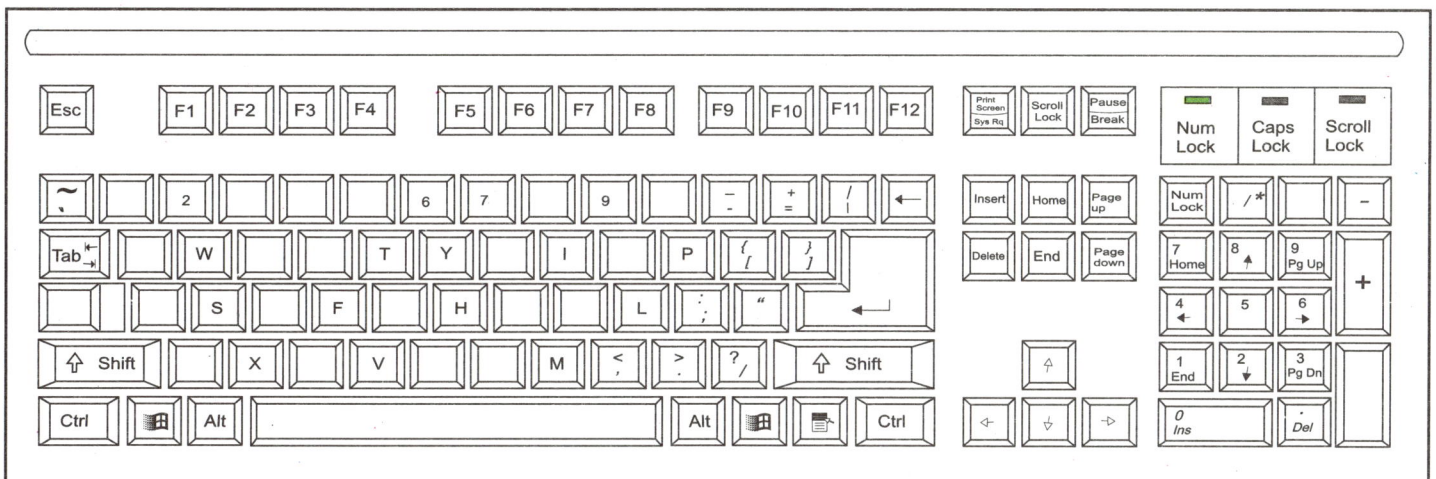

Computers—Our Lifeline-1

BRAIN TEASER

Tick [✓] the correct answer.

a.   The keys used to type your school name.

   1.   Number ☐   2.   Alphabet ☐

b.   The keys used to type your age.

   1.   Enter ☐   2.   Number ☐

c.   The key used to erase a character.

   1.   Backspace ☐   2.   Caps Lock ☐

d.   How many Alphabet keys are there on the keyboard?

   1.   11 ☐   2.   26 ☐

e.   How many Number keys are there on the keyboard?

   1.   10 ☐   2.   11 ☐

f.   How many Enter keys are there on the keyboard?

   1.   2 ☐   2.   4 ☐

g.   How many Backspace keys are there on the keyboard?

   1.   3 ☐   2.   1 ☐

2. Colour the correct key.

a. This key is also called return key.

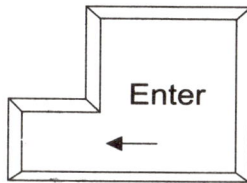 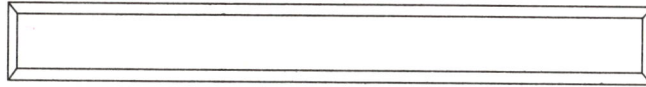 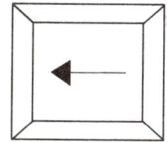

b. A key used to erase words.

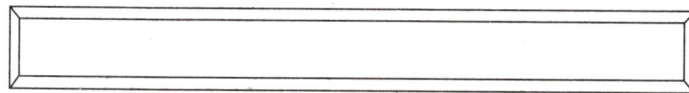 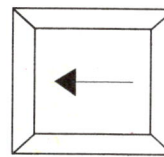 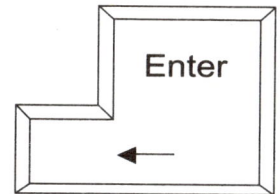

c. A key used to type your name in capital letters.

 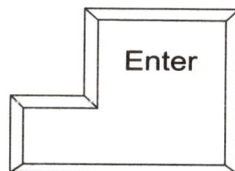 

3. Name the following keys:

a.

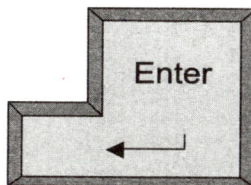

b.

4. Fill in the blanks by unscrambling the words given below.

a. To type in the computer, you need a _____

K E D O B A R Y

b. The _____ keys are used to type words.

H E A L B T A P

c. The _____ keys are used to type your age.

M U N R B E

d. The Enter key is also called _____ key.

T R R E N U

e. The _____ keys are used to type capital or small letters.

K P C S A O C L

5. Match the following:

a.	Alphabet keys	1.	ON and OFF
b.	Number Keys	2.	Typing on the computer
c.	Keyboard	3.	Eraser
d.	Caps Lock	4.	26
e.	Backspace key	5.	10

So kids ! you got familiar with the keyboard. Now I shall make you familiar with my another part - Mouse.

Hey ! look at me. I am mouse.

Why are you called mouse?

Because my **shape** and **size** look like that of a real mouse. I have **buttons** like the **ears** and **wire** like a **tail**.

Oh yes! You are very much true.

A mouse also has its own use. Now, I shall tell you about it.

MOUSE

○ A mouse is a **pointing device**.

○ It is used to **select** things on the monitor.

○ It is used for **drawing** pictures.

○ It is also used to **play** games.

Features of Mouse

○ A mouse has **two buttons** and one small **wheel**. Wheel is called **scroll button**.

○ These buttons are pressed to operate the mouse.

○ It has a **long wire** attached to it, which looks like the tail of a real mouse.

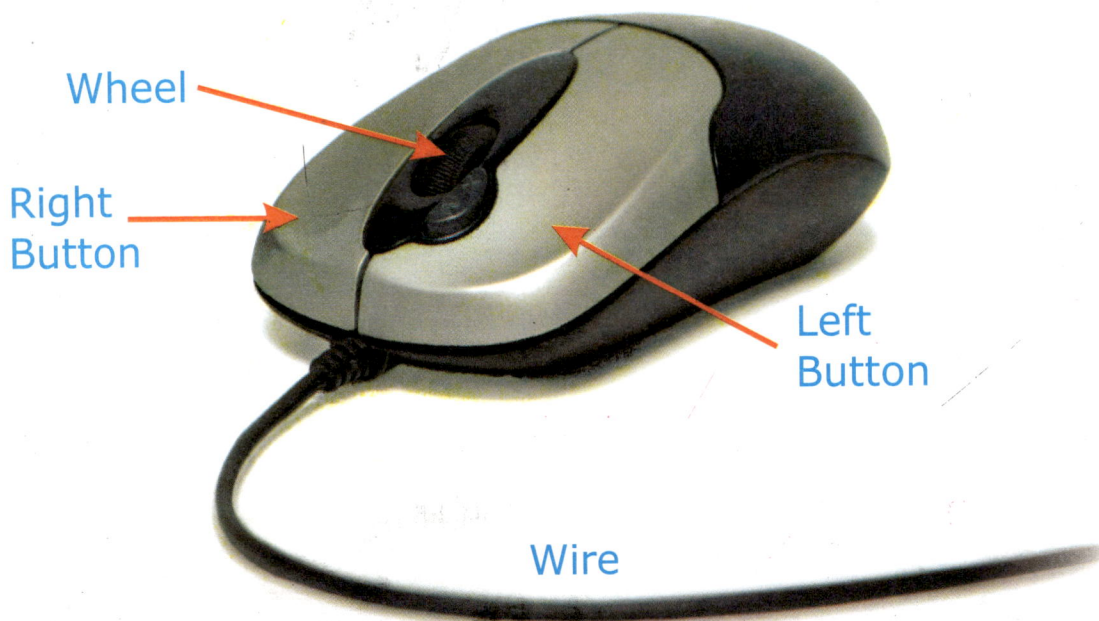

Wheel
Right Button
Left Button
Wire

HOW TO HANDLE A MOUSE

- Keep your **palm** on the mouse.

- Keep your **index finger** on the **left** mouse button.

- Keep your **middle finger** on the **right** mouse button.

- Hold the sides of the mouse with your **thumb** on one side and the **ring finger** and the **little finger** on the other sides.

- You can use the scroll button with your **index finger**.

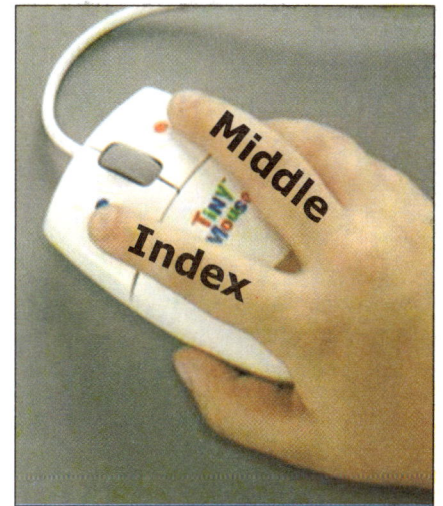

Place the mouse on the **mouse pad**.

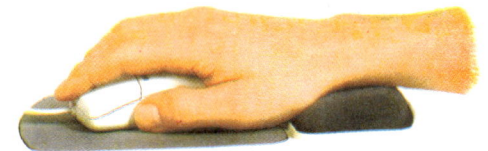

USING A MOUSE

You can use me by **clicking** my buttons.

You can operate me in different ways by using different types of **clicking**.

Remember: Pressing the mouse button is called **clicking**.

There are different types of clicking to perform different operations by mouse.

Single-click

Pressing a **left** mouse button only **once** is called **single-click**.

Single-click is used to select an object.

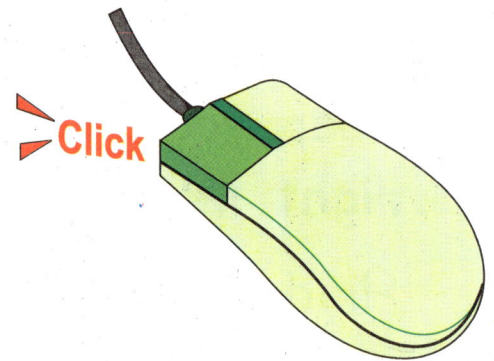

Double-click

Pressing the **left** mouse button **two times quickly** is called **double-click**.

Double-click is used to open any program like Paint or WordPad.

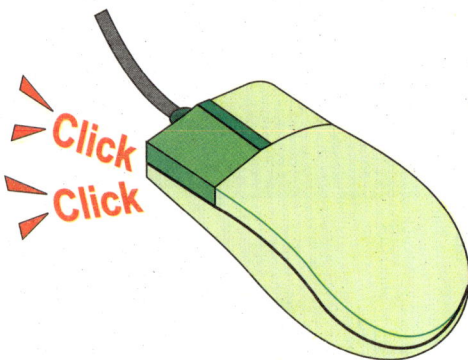

Right-Click

Pressing the **right** mouse button **once** is called **Right-Click**.

Right-click is used to display a shortcut menu.

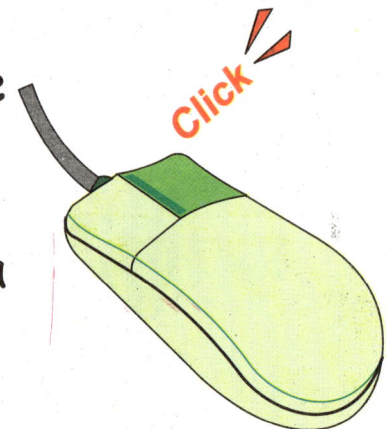

Dragging

By keeping the **left** mouse button pressed while moving the mouse is called **dragging**.

Dragging is used to move the object or draw any shape with the mouse.

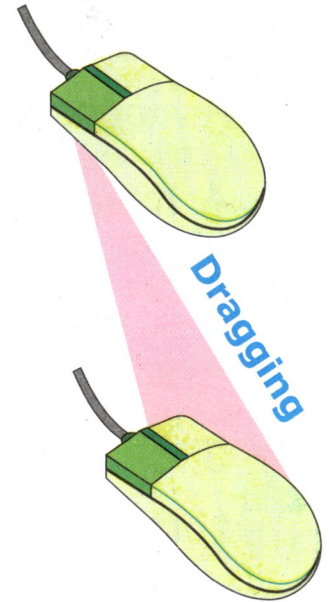

MOUSE POINTER

Mouse pointer is a **small arrow** moving on the screen of the monitor.

When you move the mouse, a small arrow also moves on the screen of the computer. This small arrow is known as **mouse pointer**.

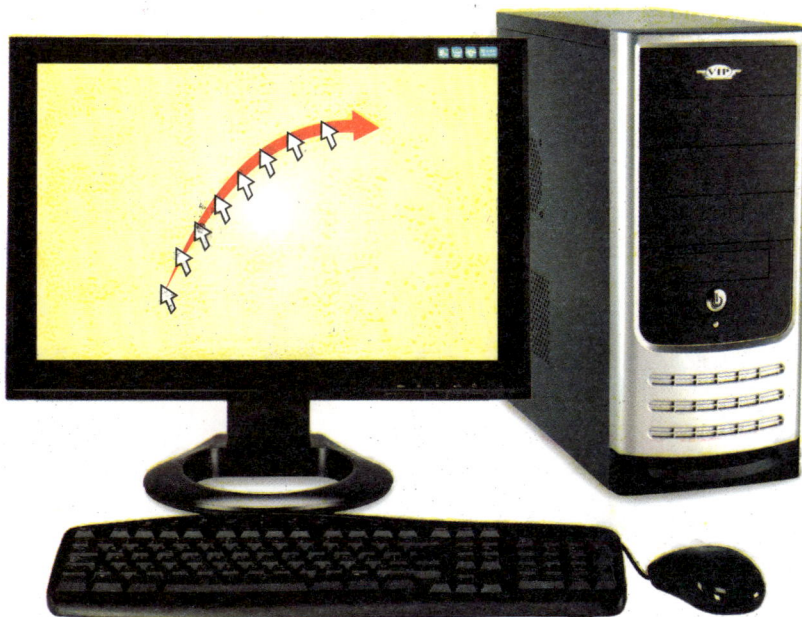

Mouse Pointer

LET'S HAVE A LOOK

○ A mouse is a pointing device.

○ A mouse is used to select the things on a computer.

○ A mouse possesses two buttons and a small wheel.

○ A small arrow on the screen is called mouse pointer.

○ Clicking, Double-click, Right-click and Dragging are the four movements of a mouse.

BRAIN TEASER

1. **Write the first letter of the picture and find the word.**

a.

M				

b.

c.

2. Complete the following words:

a. M [ ] U [ ] E

b. D [ ] A [ ] G [ ] N [ ]

c. [ ] L [ ] K [ ] N G

d. [ ] O [ ] S [ ] P [ ] N [ ] E R

e. D [ ] U [ ] L [ ] C [ ] [ ] K

3. Name the following:

a. Part of the computer that is used to select things

b. Pressing the mouse button

c. Pressing the mouse button twice quickly

d. Small arrow on the computer screen

e. Clicking and holding the left mouse button while moving

4. **Write 'T' for the true statements and 'F' for the false ones in the boxes.**

a. A mouse is used to draw pictures. ☐

b. A mouse is a useful part of the computer. ☐

c. A mouse has four buttons. ☐

d. Pressing and releasing the left mouse button is called double-click. ☐

e. We keep the index finger on the left mouse button. ☐

LAB ACTIVITY

1. Take students to the lab and show them every action of the mouse and its use.

2. Do a lot of practice to learn the use of the mouse.

3. Paste or draw the pictures of a real mouse and a computer mouse.

Real Mouse   **Computer Mouse**

FORMATIVE ASSESSMENT - 3
Chapters 5 and 6

A. Label the parts of the keyboard.

_____   _____   _____

_____   _____   _____

b. Tick [✓] the correct key.

1. C.......MPUTER   O ☐   Q ☐

2. 5 ...... 5 = 10   + ☐   − ☐

3. MOU......E   S ☐   A ☐

4. KEY......OARD   V ☐   B ☐

5. MONIT.......R   O ☐   N ☐

Dear kids, now you are familiar with my different parts and you can start working on the computer. For this purpose, you should know how to turn ON/OFF the computer.

TURNING ON COMPUTER

A computer is an **electronic machine** which works on **electricity**. So, to work with the computer, it is necessary to **Switch On** the computer.

Follow the step-by-step procedure to **turn on** the computer.

Step 1. Switch On the main **Power button** from the electric switch board.

Step 2. Switch On your **UPS** (Uninterrupted Power Supply).

Step 3. Switch On the power button available on **CPU**.

Step 4. Switch On the **Monitor** by pressing the button available on it.

The **Windows Welcome** screen appears.

You may be prompted to enter the **password**. *You can ask the password from your teacher.*

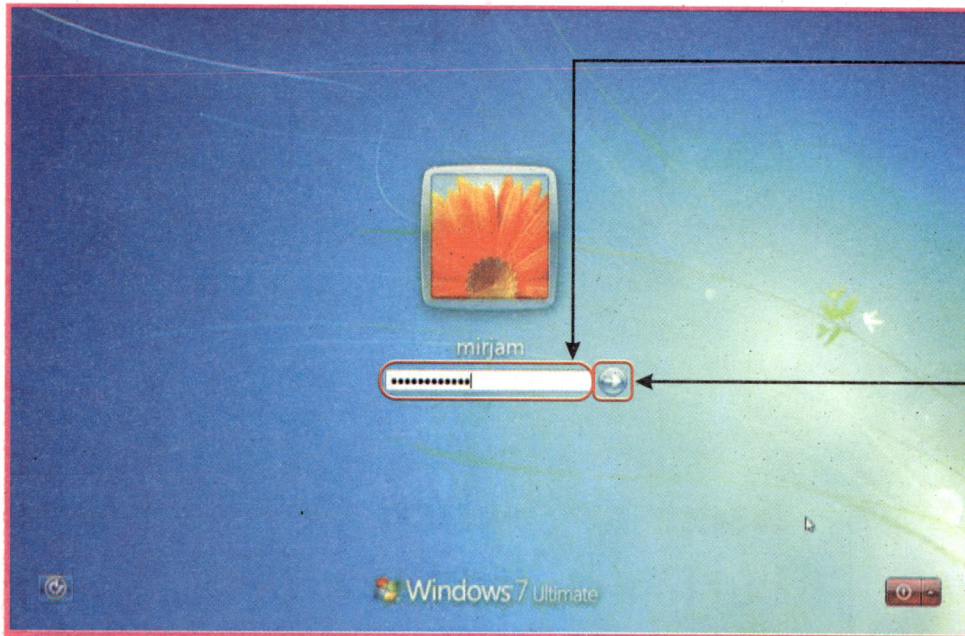

Step 5. Type the **password**.

Step 6. Click on the **Go** arrow.

Now, you will get the final desktop screen.

Desktop

Your computer is now ready to work.

Desktop: The very first screen that appears.

TURNING OFF COMPUTER

After finishing your work, you have to **Turn Off** the computer so that it may also take some rest.

To turn OFF the computer, there is also a **step-by-step procedure**. Follow the steps to turn Off the computer.

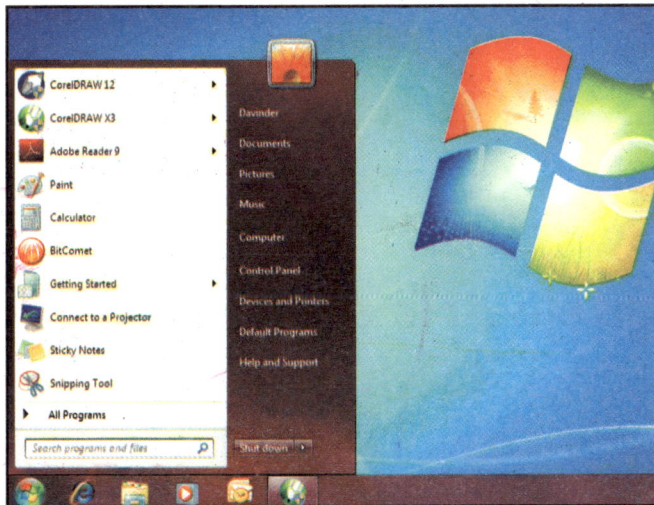

Step 1. Click on **Start** button.

The start menu will appear.

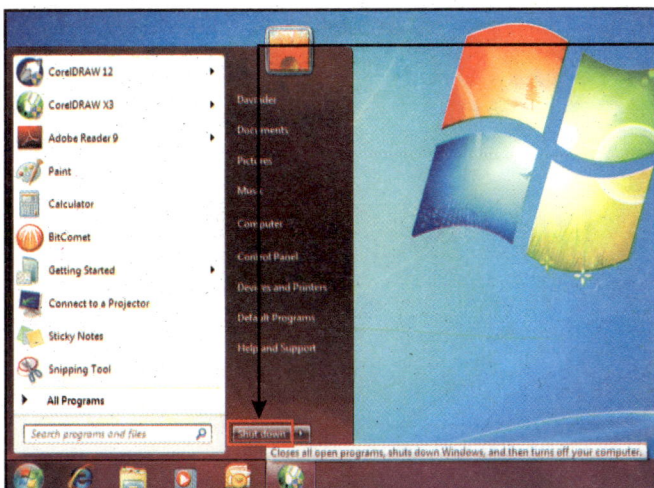

Step 2. Click on **Shut Down**.

Windows shuts down and turns off the computer.

Step 3. Turn Off the **power button** of the monitor to turn off the monitor.

Step 4. Switch Off the **UPS** **button**.

Step 5. Switch Off the **main power** from electric switch board.

You should always follow these steps to switch On/Off the computer.

Now get up and go to the computer room to try this.

Note : Never switch off the computer directly.

LET'S HAVE A LOOK

o To turn ON and OFF the computer, you should follow a step-by-step procedure.

o After finishing your work, you should turn OFF your computer properly.

o Never turn OFF the computer directly from CPU.

BRAIN TEASER

1. **Rearrange the steps to turn ON the computer properly.**

Step: Turn On the Monitor.　　　☐

Step: Welcome screen appears.　　　☐

Step: Turn On the UPS.　　　☐

Step: Switch On the CPU.　　　☐

Step: Turn ON power switch from board　　　☐

Step: Desktop screen appears　　　☐

2. **Fill in the blanks to Turn OFF the computer properly.**

(1)

_ _art bu _ _on

(2)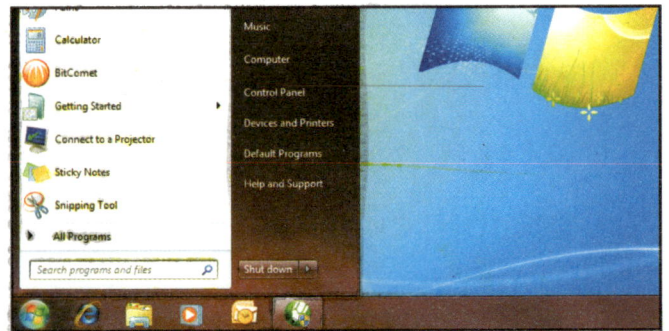

Sh_ _ D_ _n

(3)

Moni_ _ r

(4)

_ _S

(5)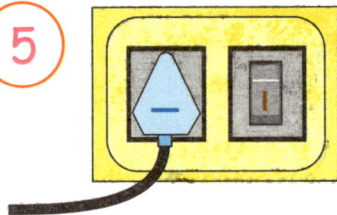

Ma_ _ Po_ _r

3. **Write 'T' for true and 'F' for false in the boxes:**

a. We should Switch Off the computer directly. ☐

b. The Computer functions without electricity. ☐

c. Turn On/Off is not a step-by-step procedure. ☐

d. You enter the password in the desktop screen. ☐

4. Tick (✓) the correct option.

a. What is the first step to start the computer?

    1. Switch On the Monitor   ◯

    2. Switch On the main power   ◯

    3. Switch On the UPS   ◯

b. What is the first step to Switch Off the computer?

    1. Click on the Start button   ◯

    2. Switch Off the main power   ◯

    3. Click on Shut Down.   ◯

c. The screen displayed after starting the computer is called

    1. CPU ◯   2. Desktop ◯   3. Icon ◯

LAB ACTIVITY

Visit your computer lab and learn the proper method of Turning On and Off the computer.

Friends, now you have learnt to Turn On/Off the computer. Let's move ahead and have some fun with it. In this chapter you will learn how to draw and colour in the computer.

MS-PAINT

Children, you use a pencil, an eraser, colours, etc. to draw on **paper**.

Similarly, you need all these things to draw in the **computer** as well. All these things are present in a program called **MS-Paint**.

MS-Paint is a program in a computer that is used to draw and paint.

STARTING PAINT PROGRAM

First Turn On your computer and then follow the given steps to start Paint.

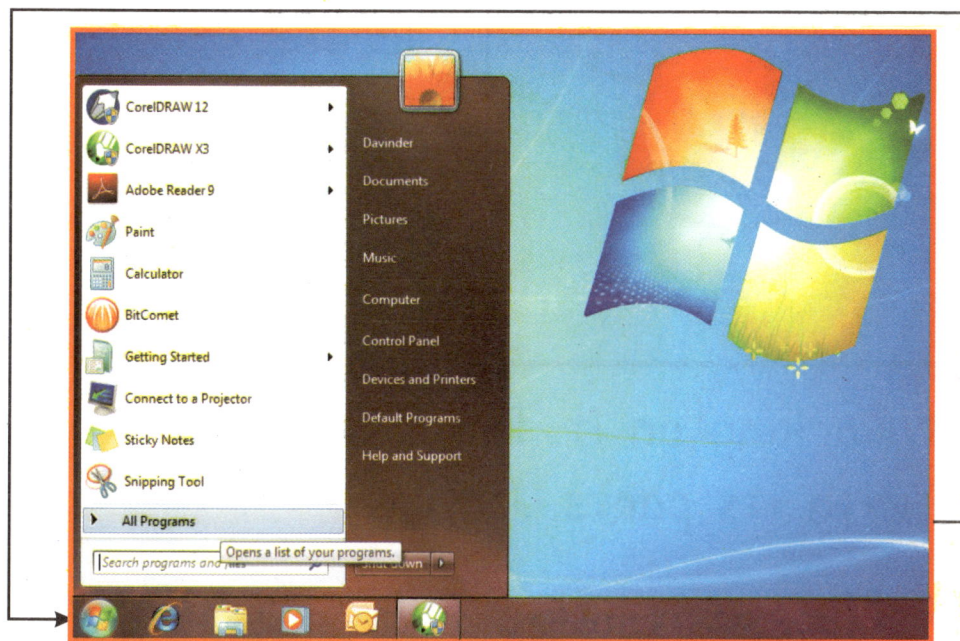

Step 1.
Click on the **Start** button.

Step 2.
Click on **All Programs.**

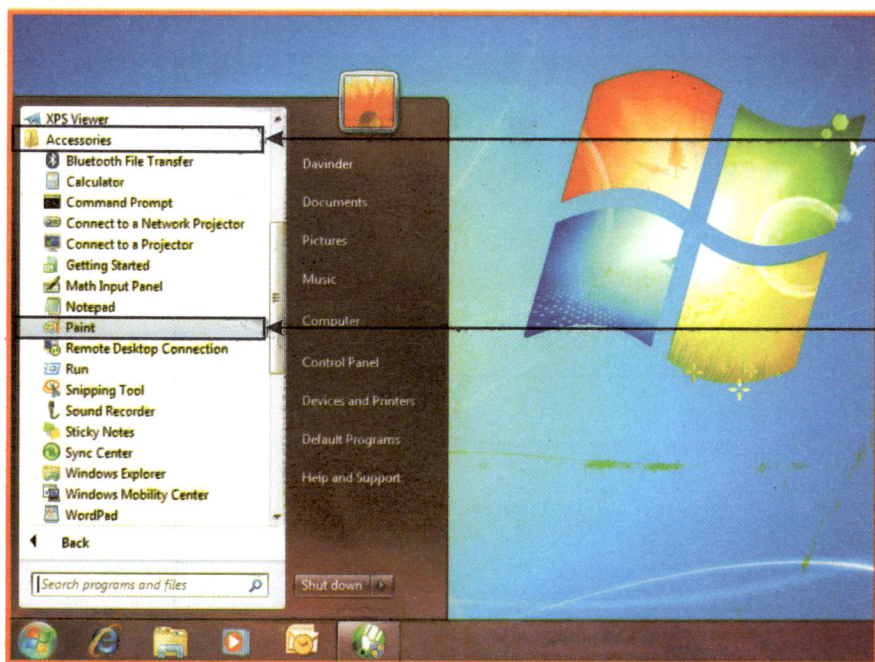

Step 3.
Click on **Accessories.**

Step 4.
Now click on Paint.

Click means pressing the left mouse button once.

Computers—Our Lifeline-1

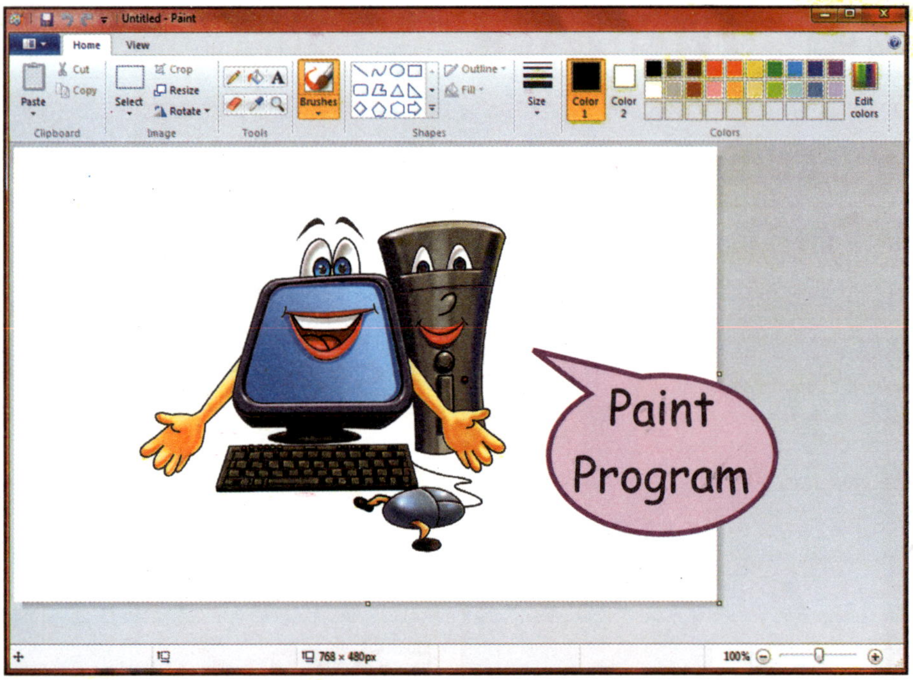

The **Paint program** will appear on the computer screen.

Now you can start working on it. But before that, you should be familiar with its parts.

PAINT WINDOW

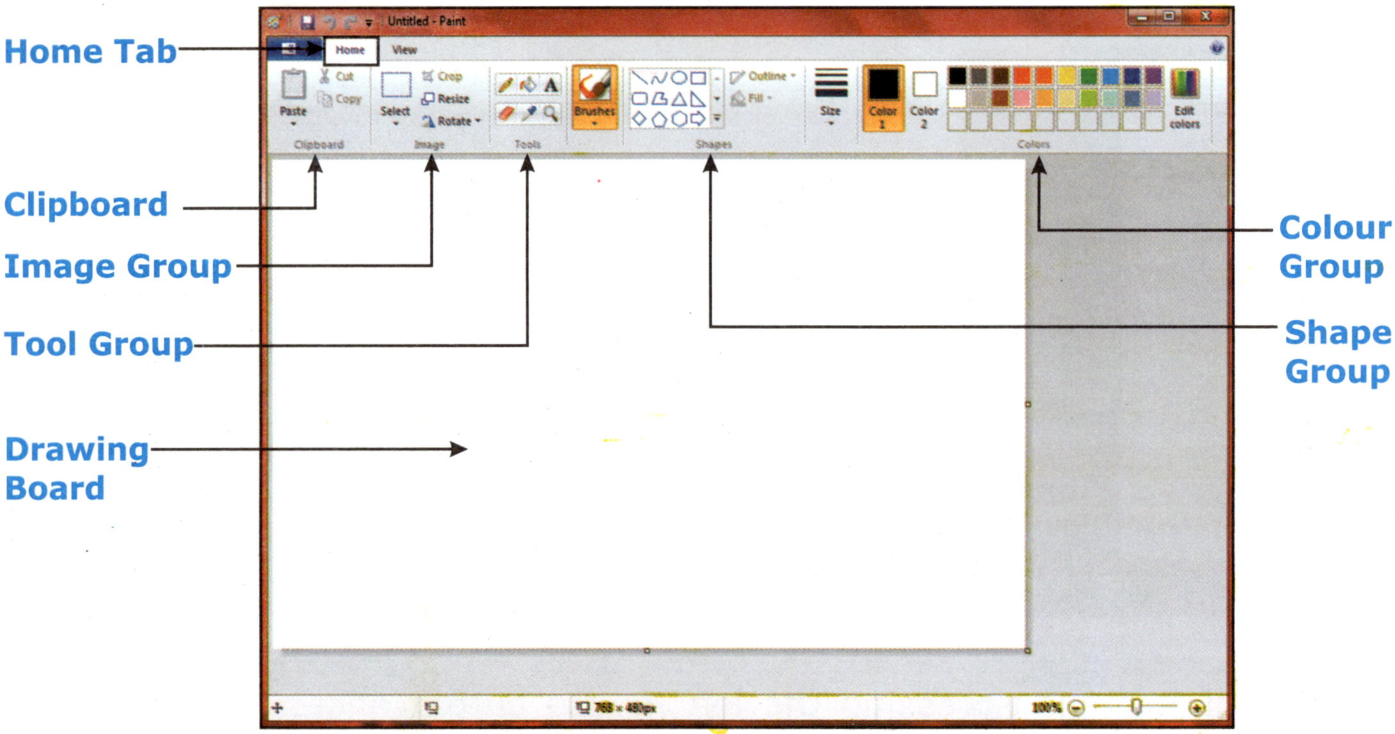

Home Tab

Clipboard

Image Group

Tool Group

Drawing Board

Colour Group

Shape Group

Clipboard

It contains various options like **Cut**, **Copy** and **Paste**.

Copy option is used to make a duplicate copy of text or picture created on the computer.

Cut option is used to move the text or picture respectively on some other place or file.

Paste option is used to place the text or picture.

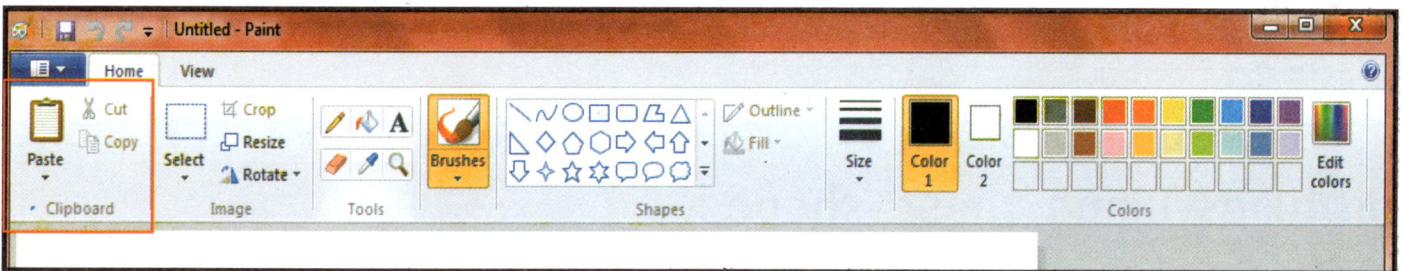

Image Group

The **Image group** contains commands to select an image and crop, resize, flip or rotate it.

We shall learn to use these commands in senior classes.

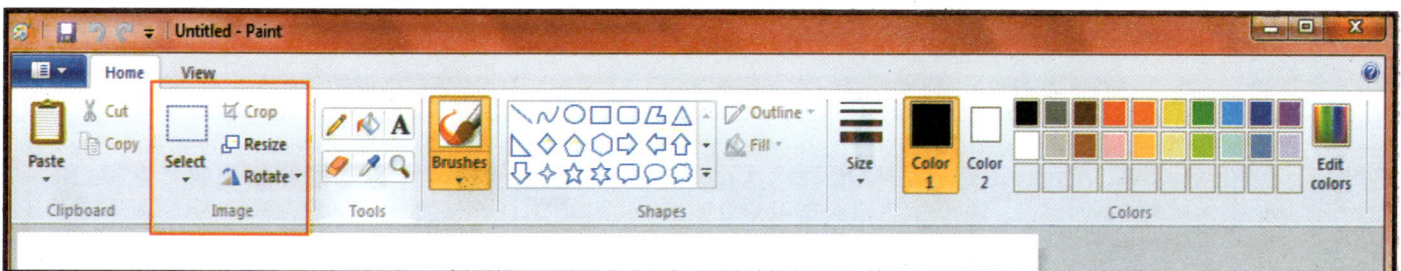

Tool Group

The Tool group contains various tools like Eraser, Pencil, Fill with colour, Eye-Droper Tool, Text Tool and Magnifier.

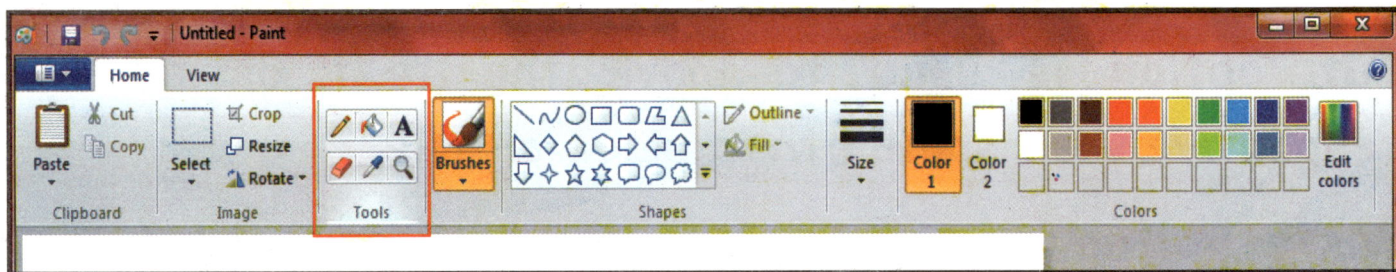

Shape Group

This group consists of different shapes. We can make pictures using these shapes.

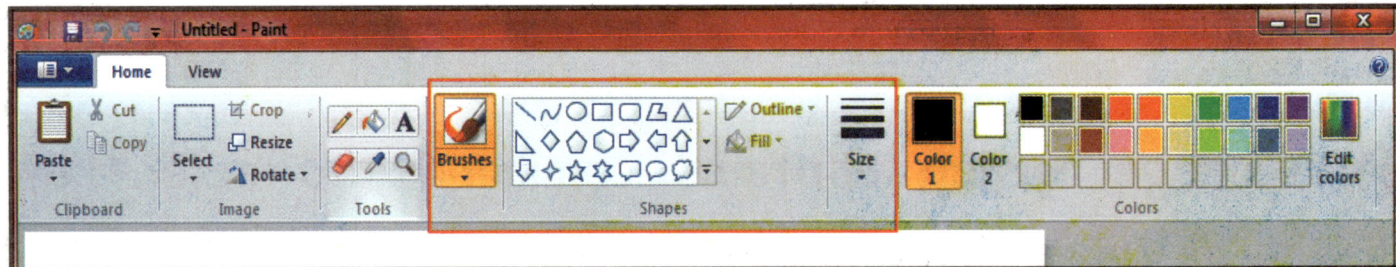

Colour Group

This group consists of different colours which are used to colour pictures.

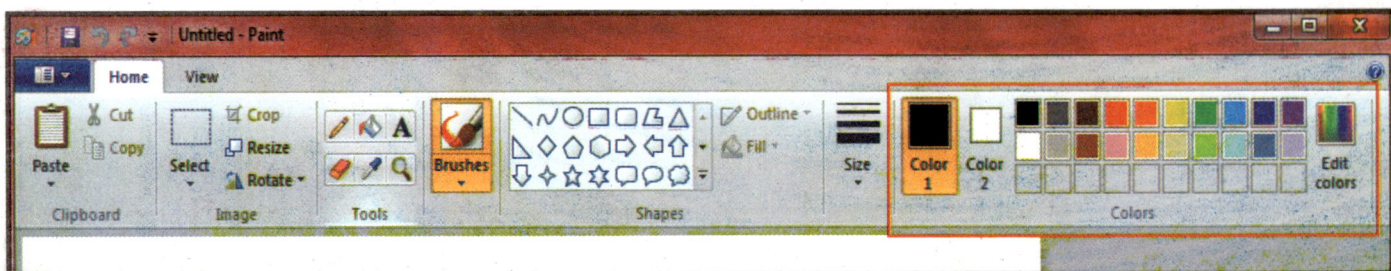

START DRAWING (USING TOOLS)

Pencil Tool

This tool provides us with a pencil to make any kind of **free-hand** drawing. You can make any shape you want with the help of **pencil tool**.

1. Click on **Home**.

2. Click on **Pencil**.

3. Click in the **Size** box.

4. Select the width of line.

5. Now on the drawing area, drag the mouse and start making drawings.

Line Tool

Line tool is used to draw straight, standing or slanting lines on the computer screen.

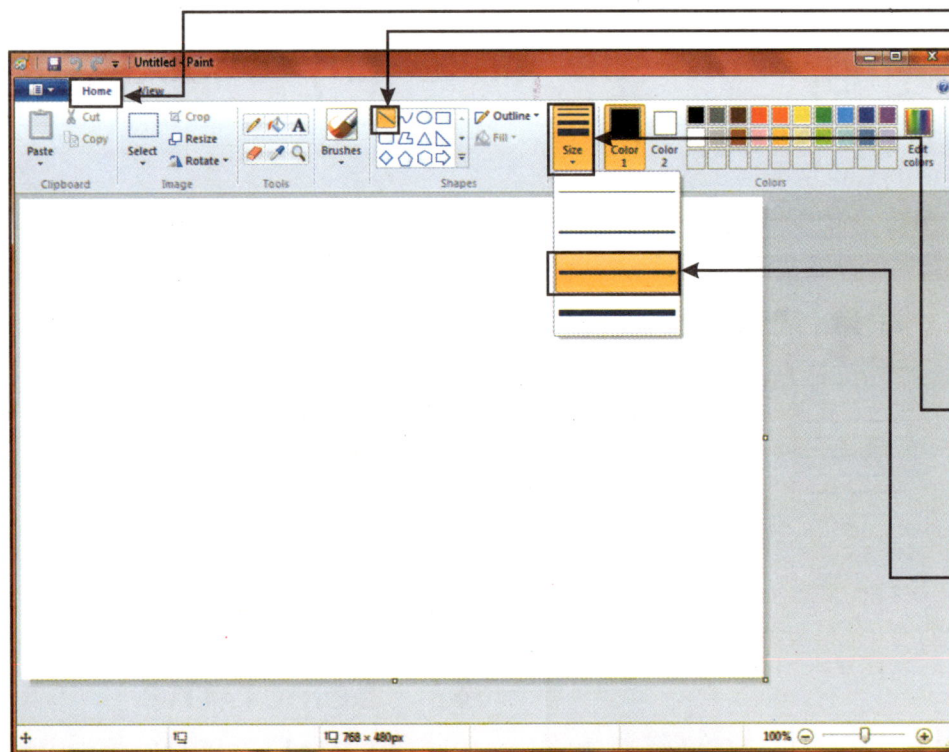

1. Click on **Home**.

2. Click on **Line** tool.

3. Click in the **Size** box.

4. Select the width of line thickness.

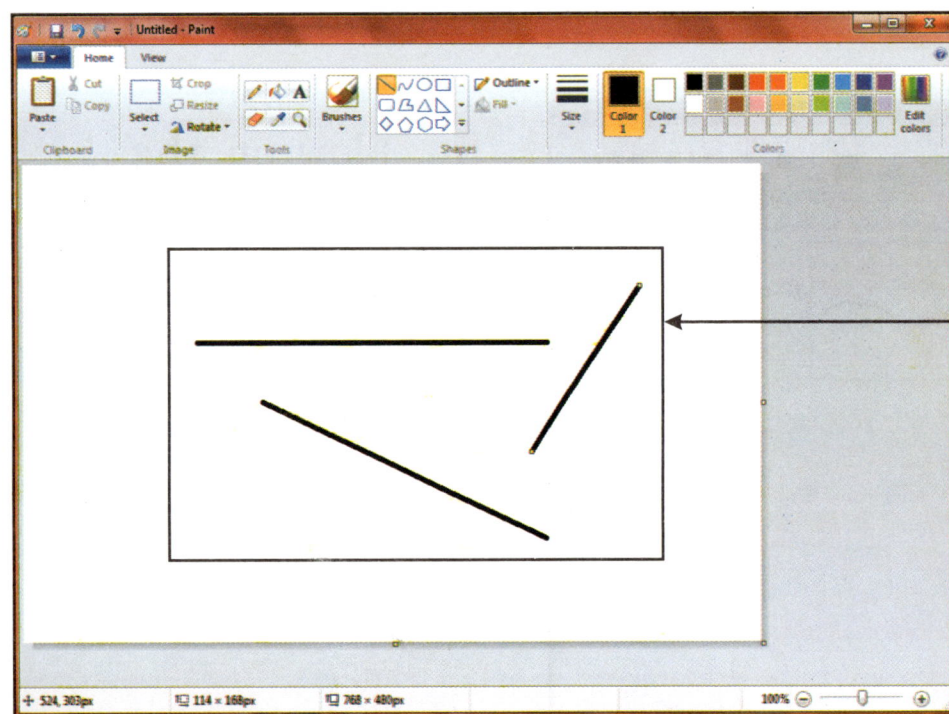

5. Drag the mouse to make a line in any direction.

Rectangle Tool

Rectangle tool is used to draw a rectangle and a square.

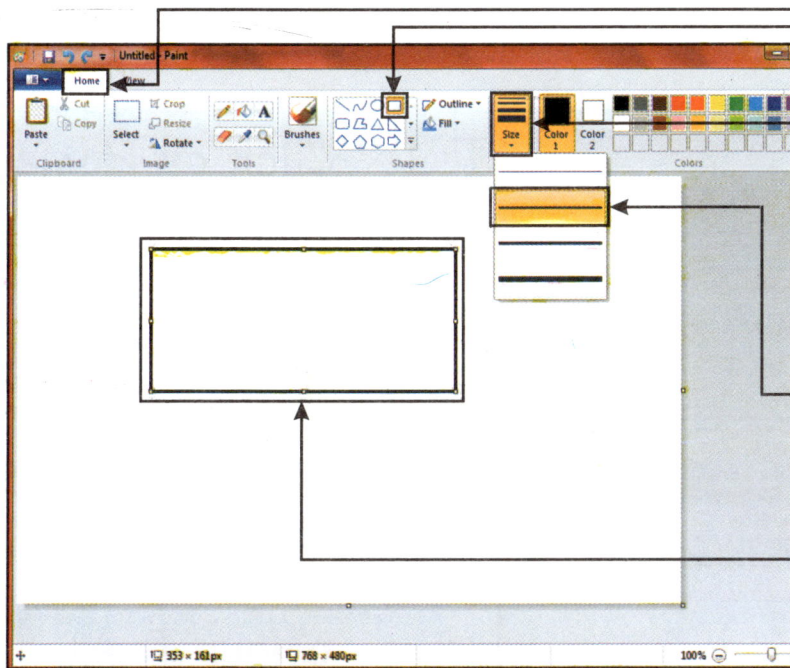

1. Click on **Home** tab.

2. Click on **Rectangle**.

3. Click in the **Size** box.

4. Select the width of line thickness.

5. Drag the mouse to make a rectangle.

Oval Tool

Oval tool is used to draw a circle and an oval.

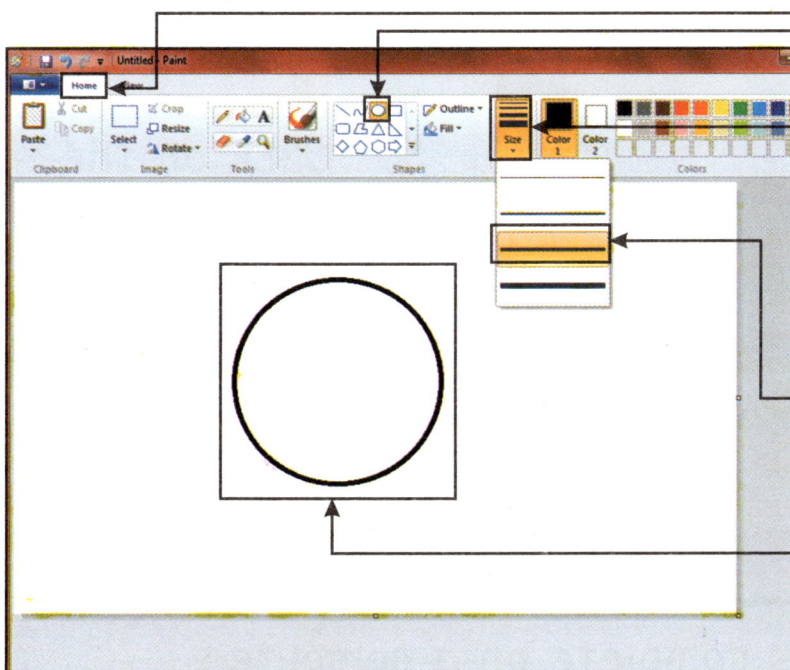

1. Click on **Home** tab.

2. Click on **Oval**.

3. Click in the **Size** box.

4. Select the width of line thickness.

5. Drag the mouse to make an oval or a circle.

Fill With Color Tool

Fill **with Color** tool is used to colour in the circle, boxes, etc. which we draw in Paint.

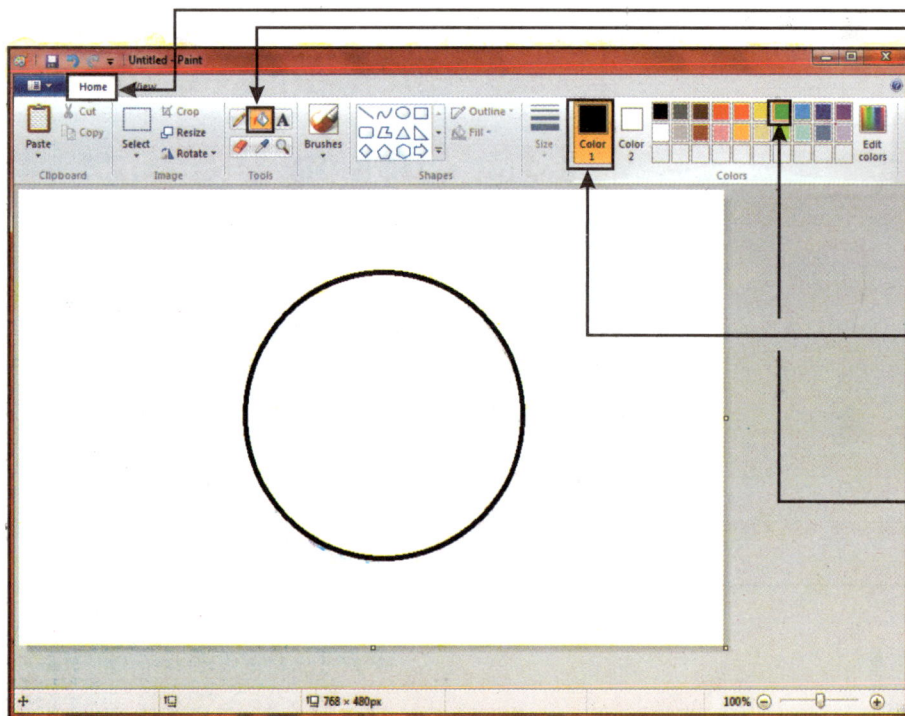

1. Click on **Home**.

2. Click on **Fill With Color**.

3. Click on **Color 1** box.

4. Click on any colour from colour palette.

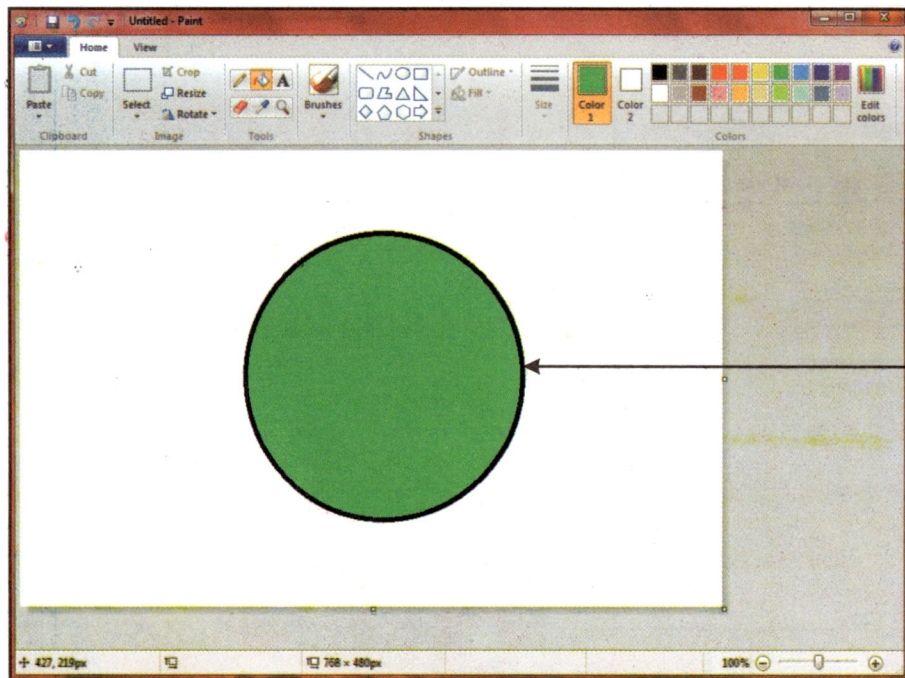

5. Click on the area where you want to colour.

Now, your colour drawing is complete on a computer.

Eraser Tool

As the real eraser, this tool is used to erase the drawn figure or a part of the drawn figure we wish to remove.

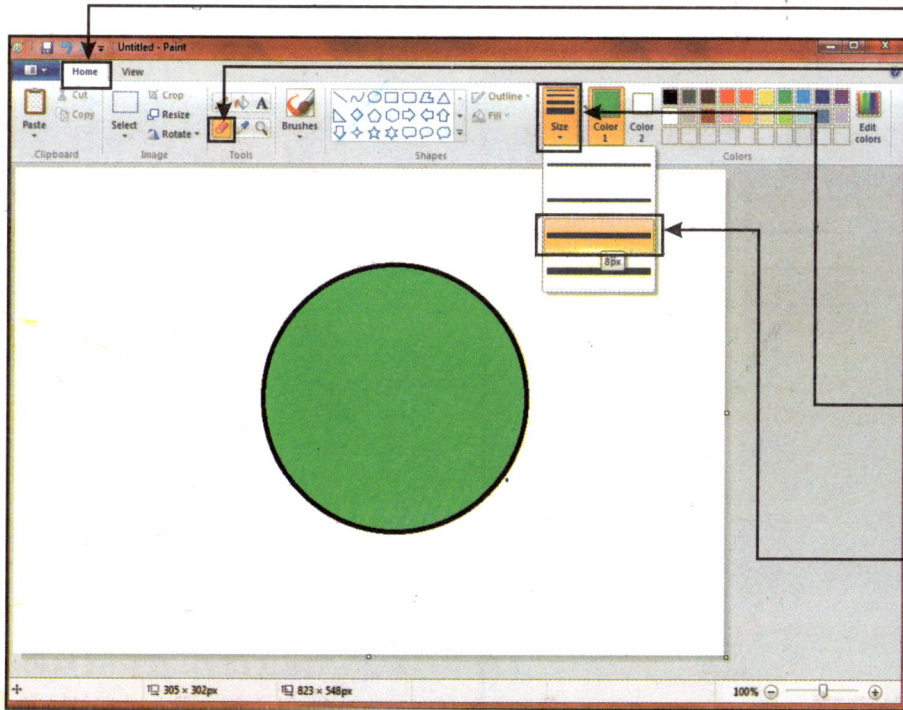

1. Click on **Home**.

2. Click on **Eraser** tool.

3. Click in the **Size** box.

4. Select the **width** of the eraser.

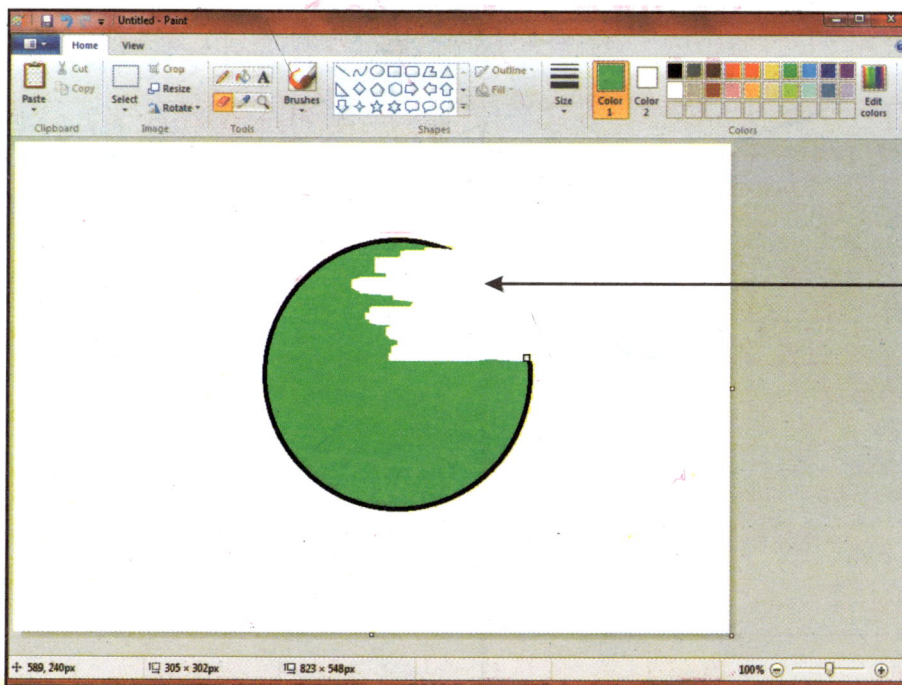

5. Drag it on your drawing in the drawing area.

Brush Tool

You can use **Brush** tool as you use a real brush in your drawing.

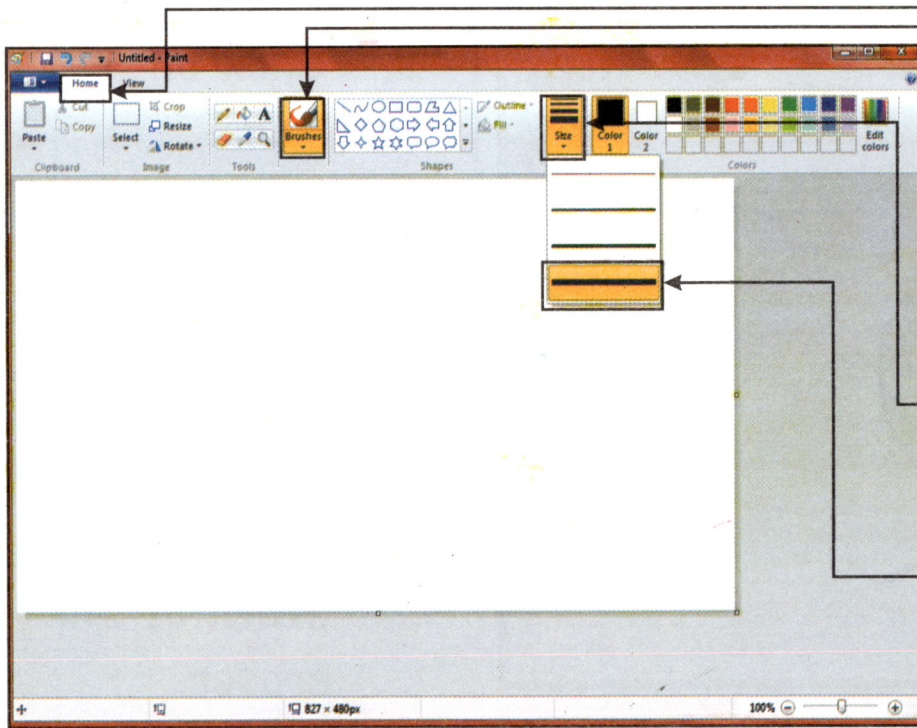

1. Click on **Home**.

2. Click on **Brushes**.

3. Click in the **Size** box.

4. Select the width of the brush.

5. Now on the drawing area, drag the mouse and start making drawings.

LET'S HAVE A LOOK

o   Paint is a program used to draw on the computer.

o   Paint has a Tool group that contains different tools to draw with.

o   Colour box is used to select the colour to be filled in the drawing.

o   Different tools are used to draw different shapes.

o   Fill with Colour is used to fill the colour in your drawing.

BRAIN TEASER

1.   Tick [✓] the correct tool.

   a.   A tool is used for drawing a straight line

   b.   A tool is used for drawing a rectangle

   c.   A tool is used for erasing the drawing

   d.   A tool is used to draw an oval

   e.   A tool is used to make a free-hand drawing

2. Write the names of the following tools.

a.

b.

c.

d.

e.

f.

3. Match the Tool names with the Tools.

Tool Name

a. Rectangle Tool

b. Oval Tool

c. Eraser Tool

d. Line Tool

e. Fill with Color Tool

f. Pencil Tool

Tool

By following the steps given below make a hut in Paint.

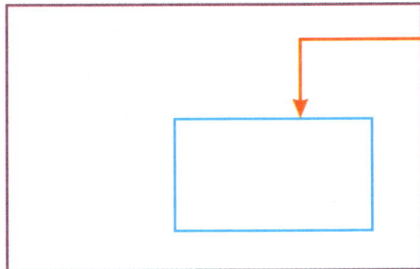

1. Click the **Rectangle** tool and drag in the drawing area to draw a rectangular shape.

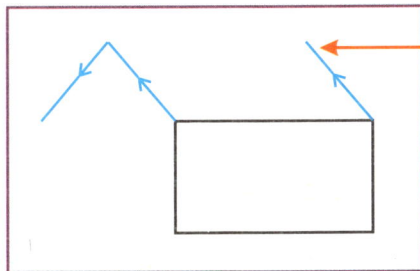

2. Now, click on **Line** tool and draw three **slanted lines** like this.

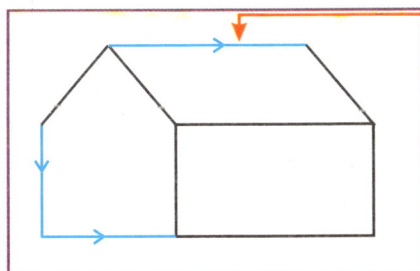

3. Using the same tool draw three **straight lines**.

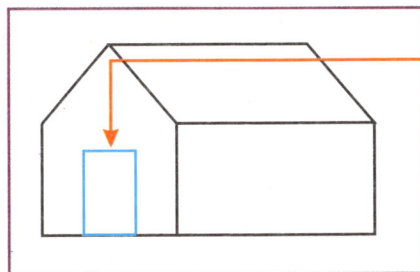

4. Take the **Rectangle** tool to draw the door area.

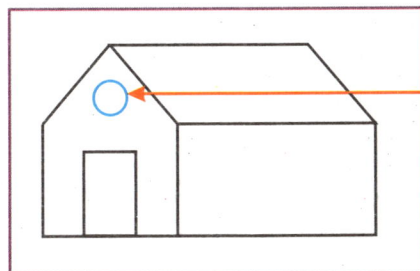

6. Now draw a small circle above the door using **Oval** tool.

FORMATIVE ASSESSMENT - 4
Chapters 7 and 8

1. Rearrange the steps to turn ON the computer properly.

   Step 1:   Switch on the monitor   ☐

   Step 2:   Welcome screen   ☐

   Step 3:   Turn on UPS   ☐

   Step 4:   Switch on CPU   ☐

   Step 5:   Turn ON power switch from board   ☐

   Step 6:   Desktop screen appears   ☐

2. Label the following:

SUMMATIVE ASSESSMENT - 2
Chapters 5 to 8

1. **Put a tick [✓] for the correct statement and a cross [×] for the incorrect one.**

a. A Keyboard has two keys on it.   [ ]

b. Enter key is used to type capital letters.   [ ]

c. A Mouse is a pointing device.   [ ]

d. Paint is used to draw shapes in the computer. [ ]

2. **Who am I?**

a. I am a small arrow on the computer screen.

I am a _____

b. I can fill colours in the object.

I am a _____

c. I can make a free-hand drawing.

I am a _____

PICTURE GLOSSARY

A Abacus

It is a very old calculating device

B Backspace Key

Backspace

Last key in the row of number keys on keyboard

C CPU (Central Processing Unit)

The brain of computer which controls and carries out all operations

D Desktop

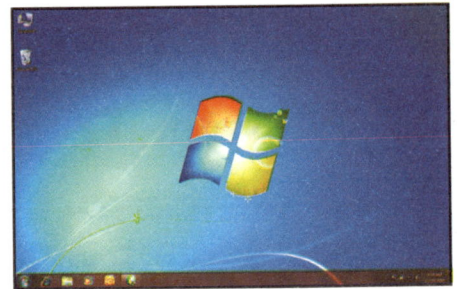

The very first screen that appears on monitor

E E-mail

A message sent electronically from one computer to another

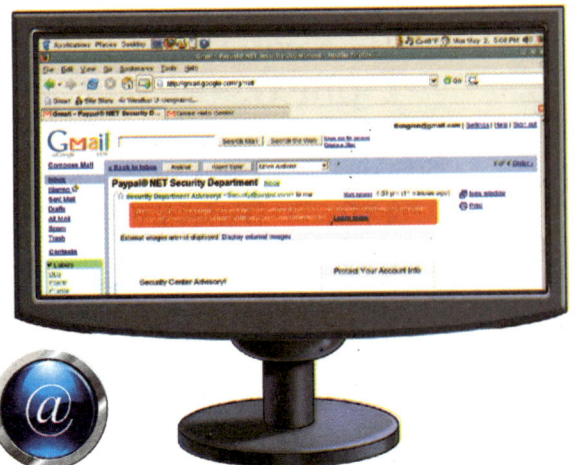

F Floppy

A magnetic disk used for storing small data

G Games

For fun and entertainment

H Hard Disk

A magnetic disk used for storing a large amount of data

I Internet

It gives us information from all over the world

J Joystick

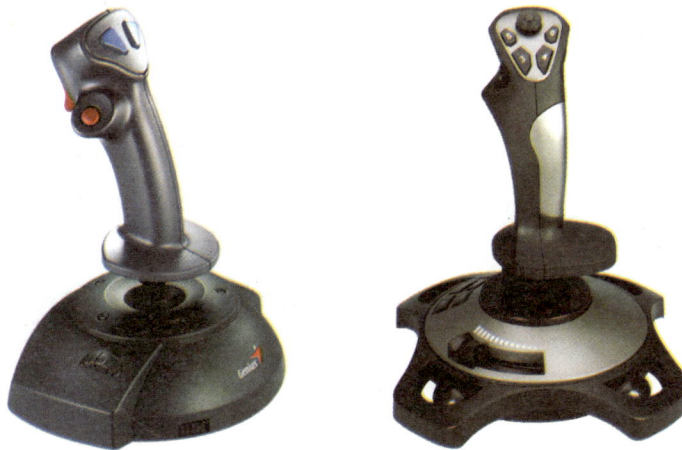

It is a device used for playing games on computer

K
Keyboard

A device that lets you type in computer

L
Laptop

A portable computer

M
Mouse

Controls cursor movements on a computer screen

N
Network

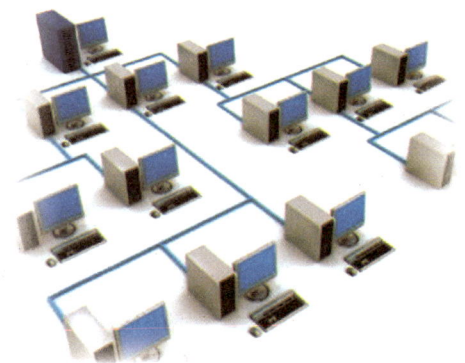

A number of interconnected computers, operations, etc.

O
Output

Result

SCORE: 31 MOVES IN 21.95s

ORION
TARGET: 31 MOVES IN 30s
MOVES: 31
UNDO: 0

OTHER STARS ← RETRY → LEPUS

The final result given by the computer

P

Printer

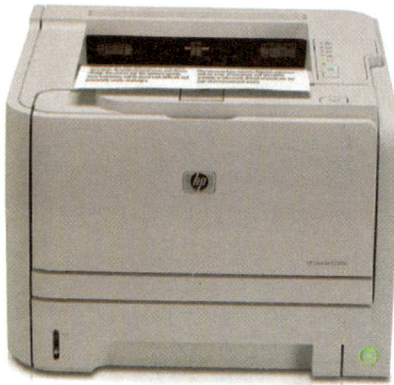

Helps to take printouts of the work done

Q

Quit

Coming out of the computer program

R

RAM

(Random Access Memory) computer memory wherein data can be read and written by CPU and other devices

S

Scanner

Scans documents and converts them into digital form

T

Trackball

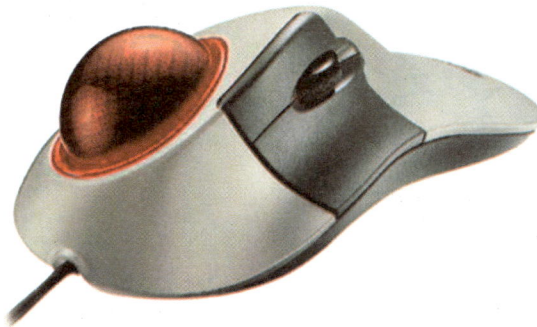

A small ball beneath the mouse helps to move a cursor on a computer screen

U UPS

Helps to do work even without main power

V VDU

Visual Display Unit, also called monitor, helps to display information

W Windows

An operating system software from Microsoft

X XP

The latest version of Microsoft Windows and Microsoft Office

Y Yahoo

A popular Website

Z Zoom

To enlarge a picture or text